COLOR
DOCUMENTARY

COLOR
DOCUMENTARY

BY LUANN KEENER

CALYX Books □ Corvallis, Oregon

The publication of this book was supported with grants from the National Endowment for the Arts, the Lannan Foundation, and the Oregon Arts Commission.

Cover art, Colorado Aspens, *by Kathleen Flannigan.*
Cover and book design by Cheryl McLean.

CALYX Books are distributed to the trade through **Consortium Book Sales and Distribution, Inc., St. Paul, MN 1-800-283-3572.**

CALYX Books are also available through major library distributors, jobbers, and most small press distributors including: Airlift, Bookpeople, Inland Book Co., Pacific Pipeline, and Small Press Distribution. For personal orders or other information write: CALYX Books, PO Box B, Corvallis, OR 97339, (503) 753-9384, FAX (503) 753-0515.

∞

The paper in this book meets the guidelines for permanence and durability of the Committee on Production Guidelines for Book Longevity of the Council on Library Resources and the minimum requirements of the American National Standard for the Permanence of Paper for Printed Library Materials Z38.48-1984.

Library of Congress Cataloging-in-Publication Data
Keener, LuAnn, 1954-
    Color documentary / by LuAnn Keener
        p. cm.
    Poetry.
    ISBN 0-934971-40-4 (cl) : $21.95. —ISBN 0-934971-39-0 (pbk.):
$11.95.
    I. Title.
PS3561.E3723C65 1994
811'.54—dc20   94-19651
                                            CIP

Printed in the U.S.A.
9 8 7 6 5 4 3 2 1

ACKNOWLEDGMENTS

The author gratefully acknowledges the following publications in which some of the poems in this volume first appeared.

ASHA, Journal of the American Speech-Language-Hearing Association: "Echolalia"; *Calapooya Collage:* "Winter Sunlight"; *The Cape Rock:* "Marine Iguana" and "Color Documentary"; *The Chariton Review:* "Kampuchea" (as "Cambodia"); *The Charlotte Poetry Review:* "Icarus Swims"; *The Greensboro Review:* "Night Watch..." and "The Bridge"; *Louisiana Literature:* "Sonogram" and "Sumeria"; *Louisville Review:* "On the Lower Surface"; *The Madison Review:* "The Man Beneath the Tundra" and "Elephant at the Washington Zoo"; *Maryland Poetry Review:* "River Dolphins..."; *The Montana Review:* "It Is April"; *New Mexico Humanities Review:* "Snake" and "Naps"; *New Orleans Review:* "Security"; *Nimrod:* "Upon the Waters" and "Thread"; *Northwest Review:* "Your Name Means Bitter Light" and "Sabra, Shatila, Beirut"; *Plainswoman:* "Anniversary"; *Poetry Northwest:* "The Bright Arcs"; *Poetry NOW:* "Cutting Bulls" (as "Mortality"); *St. Andrews Review:* "Vigil"; *Southern Humanities Review:* "Daphne"; *Southern Poetry Review:* "The Caller" (as "Drowning the Caller") and "The Manatees"; *The Sow's Ear:* "Leonardo: *The Adoration*" and "Van Eyck: *The Arnolfini Wedding Portrait*"; *Sulphur River:* "A Swallow Dives" (as "Untitled") and "Mimosa."

"Color Documentary," a chapbook containing many of the poems in this volume, appeared in *Troika III* in May 1992 from Thorntree Press, Winnetka, IL.

Excerpt from "You, Andrew Marvell," COLLECTED POEMS 1917-1982 by Archibald MacLeish. Copyright (© 1985) by The Estate of Archibald MacLeish. Reprinted by permission of Houghton Mifflin Co. All rights reserved.

Excerpt from "Rent House," in *Beholdings,* by Betty Adcock. Copyright © 1988 by Betty Adcock. Used with permission of Louisiana State University Press.

"Fish" by D.H. Lawrence, from THE COMPLETE POEMS OF D.H. LAWRENCE, Edited by V. de Sola Pinto & F. W. Roberts. Copyright © 1964, 1971 by Angelo Ravagli and C.M. Weekley, Executors of the Estate of Frieda Lawrence Ravagli. Used by permission of Viking Penguin, a division of Penguin Books USA Inc.

Kenneth Rexroth *Selected Poems,* © 1950 by Kenneth Rexroth. Reprinted by permission of New Directions Publishing Corporation.

Excerpt from "Final Soliloquy of the Interior Paramour," from COLLECTED POEMS OF WALLACE STEVENS by Wallace Stevens, Copyright © 1951 by Wallace Stevens. Reprinted by permission of Alfred A. Knopf, Inc.

CONTENTS

for my mother and father:

Mary Helen Keener
Thomas Clayton Keener

and for Luke

how the self, amazed, swam up like bone
through the lost landscape ....
—Betty Adcock

I

COLOR
DOCUMENTARY

The Manatees

Mistaken for mermaids by the lustful Spanish
because of their pendulous breasts, and one
"Hernandez" was impressed by their mental acumen—
yet, "the species could not even be called
alert. A large, phlegmatic browser of submerged
herbage...cleft-faced, wrinkled, and bristled..."

the manatees

        in their blue drowse.
The huge rubbery slugs of their bodies
whirl before the camera
just under the surface where light silvers
the aquamarine. Elephant fetuses,
ghost submarines, gentle dream cartoon.
What lovers could be more intimate than these,
blunt snout nuzzling moss-dappled back,
or these in their revolving waltz, face to face:
flippers extended, their ancient fingertips
touch. Delicacy clothed in such heavy
flesh, and singing.

       How long it is taking us
to recognize the animals: speech of the body
more articulate than ours. How long
to breach the cell of the mind, its precise walls
dividing *flesh spirit water death*
love. Now it occurs to me Odysseus

was wrong. These sirens call to us,
sailors on the bound ships,
from a world we are desperate to claim.

Marine Iguana

I didn't know his god.
—D. H. Lawrence

From the bottom of time he comes clambering up,
slinging his gladiator thighs in flat arcs,
hooked hands grappling the rocks. In his face
a look of impenetrable intelligence.

And the divers like black puma fish
revolve with their cameras. A tiny electronic ear
measures his heartbeat. They want to know
how it is done: the held lungs, navigation
at this depth. Now they chase him down,
down, until he stops. At ninety feet
the heart withdraws blood from the stilled limbs.
He turns past fear to rise, arms flattened
to his sides, swaying his oddly human shoulders.
One diver jockeys before him, face to face
like a child trying to engage a wizened adult.
The iguana turns his head aside
in polite avoidance, as you might turn
from someone who does not know your heart.
He has nothing to tell. There is no hurry.
Time is the thing

his being has understood, how to turn it
like water, dance the deliberate dance.
He climbs an unbreathable heaven
holding his breath.

Elephant at the Washington Zoo

It's you twists my heart, not the poet
in his business suit, years dead, bless him.
He never was this far from his element.
They've made a concrete pool for you.
A concrete mote substitutes for a fence.
It's ninety-eight degrees and I walk out
of the hippo house to see you bobbing and floating
in your stone bath like a huge, solemn baby.
You're batting a tire in the water, rolling over
as if you weighed nothing. How good it must feel,
all your insides buoyed in the sapphire,
chlorinated water. Does this compensate
for the elephant walks, the communal wallows,
the mysterious grand burials, bone by bone,
the vast savannah, rippling beyond recall?
Foolish question. No frail word
bridges the millennia of separation between us.
Those of us who see you from civilization's
pocked plain are dumbstruck, helpless.
You speak to *us*, with your wise, small pleasure.
Like a child playing in the dust of a bombed street,
you convict us of something terrible.

Kampuchea

Headlong into winter the cold poems churn.
I do not look for them.
Stomachs of starving mothers droop
with dead weight. I hide the notebook.

All afternoon I crack nuts, thinking
that something—thick, sweet, simple—
could fill this hunger. A tradition
one could chew and swallow. *This is my
body, broken...*

                    Feed us.

                □ □ □

The television camera closes in.
Huddled in yourself, a shock of sticks
bone against bone, you wait.
Cough is a dull blade at your throat.
You lift your head
and the folksinger leans near, gingerly
like someone examining ancient cloth.
She hums, cradling you with her voice.
This is your moment. At thirteen,
eyes flat with hunger,
you are flashed to the world.
In my living room I put down my food.
I cannot help you.

                □ □ □

For days the wasps search at the window
like small steady hands. I inspect their bodies
through the glass: abdomen, thorax,
mouth parts. Their tiny clocks
run down, slowed by cold. Today
one gets inside, falls
into sticky traps of web on the sill.
His head bobs frantically.
With a fork and a cup, I extract him
gently, deliver him
out onto dry, dry grass.

Sabra, Shatila, Beirut

The sun was white.
Barbed wire rolled its waves
around the camp. My mother
walked out of shadow
from a shop, her shawl bluer
in the sun. Ahmed
skipped beside her. Then Ahmed
dropped in a heap like a puppet,
my mother dropped
on her knees, on her face.

                                       I saw this
before I saw the red
stream from my shoulder. The guns
rattled the air, danced
in the heat faster and faster,
the red skirts of screams whirling.

The sun laid its palm
over my eyes. A ship rode far out
in the shivering heat. A child
stood on the shore, his mouth stretched
with no sound. His limbs jerked
as he danced in place.
The sun's fingers

woke me. I slept again.
On the beach the small mountain
grew and grew: arms, legs,
each looking for its brother.
The ship was smaller.

On the second day, pain twisted me.
The legs and arms breathed in the sun,
burst their sleeves. I sat up
alone. When the soldier lifted me

I screamed. *Now we must*
sit up out of our torn bodies and walk
to a new place. The white sand
stretched away.

Thread

Two days ago a young man and woman
were burned alive in a street in Chile:
their clothing, then their skin
like a wafer in the mouth of flame.
I am not

worthy, I have come out
to sit in a nook of oak scrub and pine.
The summer light is a hail of needles.
In a corner of vision, a red wasp
pursues a large spider, stings it
again and again, to paralysis.
The spider folds its legs in a bony rosette
and the wasp drags it over turf and needles,
then high into a young dogwood,
Christ's passion tree. I know it is still
alive. O what
would you have me do, how to weave
the garment from this fierce thread.

Night Watch: Titan Missile Explosion, Damascus, Arkansas, September 1980

A nuclear warhead catapults into woods:
Sirens. People scatter in the dark.
For days we sit up late. Images tumble
like all the city's bells...

The blind boy's fingers tremble, moving
across the words, small foxes terrified
to enter the clearing.

Trinca, Triolo—two immigrant cobblers
on the corner. I whisper their names
like a mantra, walking with two worn soles
in a paper sack. Trinca winks
as I hoped God would.

On TV a four-year-old girl
reads Shakespeare aloud, fears
she will die before meeting Marlon Brando.
Small fist poised over the typewriter,
she is a miracle.

The dead cardinal on the sidewalk:
blood that fell for miles
from an angel's shoulder.

And at night the chemicals wake us.
The stones in my chest will not open.
Last night I woke from a dream of bombs:

we had jumped into water to save ourselves
but you were out of sight and I knew
there was no help but to wake up.
I drank wine with aspirin, sat for hours
reading how someone traveled
Chicago to Seattle on a train,
saw moose, coal yards, snow-drifted towns,
finally the Boeing flats. He was happy. Slowly,
slowly, it calmed me.

Rain Forest

The rain forest is burning, enriching
the ground for crops.

Unknown Indians attack a farm settlement.
Of the seven children, they kill two,
sons aged nineteen and nine, and kidnap
a third. Later the farmer finds his dog,
jaws torn out of its head, the teeth
scattered. Did the Indians toss them backward
over their shoulders, conjuring trees
to spring up where they fell?
Or do they fear the farmer will sow them
to reap more sons?

The forest keeps burning.
A medium comes to console the stricken mother.
She says the Indians will not give up
the captive child: They like him. They wish
to learn his language. The forest burns.

Here is a poacher who has trapped an ocelot.
He looks at the camera, his slack face pleasantly open.
Could he make as much prospecting gold?
the reporter asks. He returns a broad grin:
Yes. But cats are easier.
The animal tries to leap, but the shut jaws
of the trap drag at one hind leg.
How does it maintain its dignified posture,
seated like a cat in a Mayan frieze?
It looks over its shoulder at the trapper,

eyes calm, oddly gentle even in fear.
The poacher has stripped a long branch,
smashes it down with a crisp snap.
Scene edit. Now he is carefully folding
the supple skin, its spots black-rimmed lakes
of gold. Are the cats dying out?
Yes, unless you go deep into the forest.

The phantom *I-gru-wu-er-wow-wow*
are at last contacted by government agents.
They must be saved from decimation by disease.
One day, intrigued with gifts of knives and metal pots,
they simply walk into the government camp.
The agents stare, stunned by their beauty.
Slim naked bodies, relaxed faces
radiate the aura of the forest.
Like it, they are very old and very young.
They finger radios, buckles, paper cups.
In minutes several youngsters are wearing T-shirts.
How fast these people will disappear! It is happening
already. The eyes of the agency men
are full of wonder and pathos. They know
they themselves are helpless, are administering
only another kind of death.

The fires are tiny squares of light flickering
on the satellite image, melting to thick patches
along the road paved by the World Bank.

The *Igruwuerwowwow* explain that the kidnapped child,
crying, was slain minutes after the battle,
buried a few hundred yards into the forest.

Water corrugates the muddy farm settlements
where the civilized live in poverty, filth, and fear.
Water has lost its trees, lost the path
of its ancient cycle. In the New Village,
Water does not know where to go.

Color Documentary

A diver crawls into a submarine
years after it collapsed like a heart
in the sea's grip. Sea flowers bloom
in the lamp beam. At the broken center
a tumble of bones embrace,
too white in this first light.
Sand pours from a jawless skull. He pulls
back along the lifeline
finning toward the surface

where it is worse, where the Teletype
never stops. Still, he bursts
through to air, is hoisted to the lap
of the ship. Salt water drains
into his eyes as he peels off
the wet suit, stands up again
alive and breakable in full light.

II

THE
BLOOD—TIE

The Blood–Tie

My grandfather lifted my grandmother up
from where she clung to stones in the dank shaft
of the well, he clinging to the rope, his small
body fear-hardened, lifted with a furious grip
up from the ice-black water her who held in one arm
their son and only child yet, first-born with
honey curls, toddler in a white dress, baby boy
who had fallen there where the packed stones' moss
was barely green in filtered light, where
water-singing had drawn him, while above their heads
the sky was a blue, bitten wafer; lifted her up,
arms welding the shrieking child to her breast,
his life theirs, and heaviest, yet light
as the caught stars in her Cherokee hair,
its stout trunk wound in his fist:
Lifted up by the thousand roots,
sinew, vessel, bone and gene, the million
filaments, the blood-tie.

Security

Late, late, all of us in bed,
me tucked down in the rollaway
watching grandfather's cigarette,
a tiny sun in deep space...
the slow river of their talk...
                              and the train
would whistle, and pass.
Nothing like it,

nothing like it since.
And yet still, no matter what,
when I hear it I am there
in the moon-white sheets, in the dark,
a whole loaf of joy rising,
rising toward morning, morning
can hardly wait.

Naps

Afternoons at my grandmother's,
sleep was a rich milk,
a thing entered into with loss of self.
Sunlight played through the chinaberries;
the conversation of hens
sifted the hours.
Sometimes she lay down with me.
The floorboards groaned when she rose.
It was loneliness, finally,

that woke me: Her thin voice,
its minor-key wordless ballads
mourning something sleep offered
that we couldn't hold.
Always I found her on the front porch,
green black-eyed peas shooting from their pods
with hard pings into the dishpan.
Around the firm, whole bread of her body
day resumed itself.

Snake

When my grandmother broke her arm
it was so much worse than the time
I saw siding sloughing off the house.
Seeing her back from the clinic,
standing, smiling, unchanged,
was a soft shock, like catching oneself
before falling. The little knob on the wrist,
set wrong by the doctor, grew back
to the side of the bone. It hurt me
like my best doll's missing thumb.

Washday, the kitchen
was a moonscape of denim mounds.
The washer chugged, digesting its blue bread.
Her large hands cranked the wringer,
feeding dark tongues into the rinse bins.
I ran out to watch the gray stream
gush from an uncoiled length of old fire hose
into the chicken yard. The chickens
were frantic, marooned by the flood
on little islands of high ground.

One afternoon
as I leaned to look out the window,
a chicken snake sunned his thick body on the sill.
In the aftermath of terror, it was worse
than the siding or the misshapen arm:
Relentless suspicion he had come
to steal something. For days I inventoried
old powder boxes, milk-eyed marbles,
dark blue unguent jars.

Mimosa

for my grandmother

What was the tree saying
that day you leaned against it
buoyed in its pillow of scent?
I was ten, I had Mother's camera.
Without knowing, I knew
to catch and hold as much of you
as I could: your body's country
losing ground, your face already
gathering shadows, the intricate arteries
turning to tunnels of fine stone
for the longest passage.
The tree hovered behind you
like a presence from another world,
each of its dark pink stars
a blur to the straining eye.
It floats now in this photograph,
lifting you in its helium aura
as you lightened toward death.

We Toil, We Spin

The fragrant barn, the pasture with its yeasty
rise, pocked by the dump ground that stopped
the creek. A green eyelash of elms hid that.
But the land was not at rest.

There under stewing sun, in the sky's
hot vise, my father is revving up
his orange truck, the churning Oliver,
the bright blue plane. He's got
to go, and I'm a step behind, running
in my cut-off jeans and dirty sneakers,
twelve years old, wound up tight.
We're both happy: we are in a hurry.
Look at the wheat like melting butter,
the combine crouched, hungry. Those white puffs
in the sky are God's glory, His eye on us.
We're pushing uphill in the heat, the good sweat
breaking.

Father, even now, even asleep,
I'm still trying hard as I can.

Puberty

Sunrise would burst
into the fields like the first
egg, light eddying
gold in the chinaberry,
its long fingers touching
the wrists of the lavender.
My windows with their pink sills,
my hardwood floor, slick with it.
And me every day new, mind
splitting its bud sheath.
The drowsy arms of the redbud
broke out in a rash of blossom.

That Saturday Morning

my mother sawed a chicken's neck
in two with a butcher knife. I hated
its screeches, its white feathers
sprayed red, the birth smell
that rose from the scalding pot.
The waxen feet, hacked off,
curled on little balls of nothing.
The soft-shelled eggs slid out
and deep in me a twinge
where the nest of microscopic suns
ripened toward pain.

That afternoon, the brown paper package
"Introducing You to a Wonderful Secret"
arrived, thick with its cottony bandage.
Handing it to me, she turned
to slicing breast from back from thighs.
Nightgowned with flour, they dropped
in grease. I went to feed

the chickens, wouldn't look
at the sky where sunset already bled.

A Swallow Dives

leveling out inches above the ground
at summer's end.

                              I hold a photograph
of my father and me, standing
in a wheat field in summer. The point then
was how high the wheat came—up to my chest,
up to his waist. Now, it is how my hair is rough
and blonde as wheat against the dark ground
of his shoulder, how one person seems to look
out of both our faces. How the picture brims
with stillness. How clearly, neither
the wheat, the rolling clouds, he nor I
could imagine the future:

                              Even the field
turned strange with other lives.
I put the picture down, notice
a fleck of gray and yellow near the edge:
Steady grace of a field lark taking flight.

Cutting Bulls

We lost a calf the other day,
a black Brahma with the royal hump.
He died of that operation which makes
guardians of those who would be kings.

The men stood in the sun laughing,
two hands and the knife glistening.
They worked joking and laughing
and we ate that light strong meat
—mixed with cracker meal.

One calf did not go to graze with the others.
In a corner of the lot he lay
bleeding, cut too deep,
while small flowers bloomed in his veins.
He died a long time.

Stretched with chin on the grass,
legs curled to his belly, they found him.
The dump truck moved monotonously with its burden
toward the woods. A shaggy ravine
swallowed him back.

The men looked solemn aside,
felt the sun's blade cut them
and did not know what to think
of the quick surety of accident
nor of how death closes swifter than water

over a stone.

Your Name Means Bitter Light

for my mother

I.
This is the story I was born into,
bigger than I was, just as you stepped through
to the other side.

That day the bubble of sanity
burst. They took you to that other
hospital, where the blue fire leapt
through your head, O in the name
of help

            it kept on having to happen.
Once when we came to get you:
the huge waiting room
with its strict tiles, black and white,
the rampant sun, and you
at the far end on a staircase
in an aqua robe, your smile
rushing toward us. *Mother*
I must have said, and it did not
comfort me, terrified as I was
by such health.

II.
            Years later
you came into my room
dragging the iron by its cord

like a balky puppy. *It won't
do the work*—the crushed bundle
of grandfather's shirts
you couldn't discard, the past
too knotted to iron out.

You forget these scenes.
When I'm home, your face hides
in its labyrinth of lines,
you stay down there, turning in sleep
from the sun's corridor.

But I walk in that chill light.
I carry you, not like a mother
but like a twin
I injured at birth.

The Bright Arcs

One of childhood's chancy afternoons
I found Mother's first wedding ring
in the chicken yard among bits of glass,
the thin gold mounting housing dust
beneath its one dull eye. The air quaked
with sunlight. Carefully I washed it
under the hydrant, then went to find her.
Without a word she shut it in a drawer.
Whose is it? I asked at the supper table.
Summer darkness slid through the windows,
bunched itself in my father's face.
Like a cloud tearing in invisible winds
another wound opened in her. We let
silence seal it. I went on growing up
with what knowing I could carry, half enough.

It's taken years to open that drawer.
Now I grasp the pull, looking for rings
that connect: my folded-down marriage
that breathes in its cedar corner as I leave
another house I can't mine or hold.
What I find are the bright arcs,
the half-rounds: how the eye sees half
the worn circle on the finger, sees it
whole when it lies empty in the palm.

III

UPON
THE WATERS

Experience

Suddenly it seemed quite clear to her
that she was most a princess just before
the prince arrived. As long as the white horse
stamped and blew in the cool woods, there was no
limit to magic. Before she pricked
blood from her human hand, the golden spindle
could not fail, the marriage could not unspool
from its cloudy castle.

                       Watching her long
finger extended to choose the wish,
she saw it fall from myth, the fairies turn
to hunched crows. And yet,
cloistered in those high turrets, that ether
of solitude, how else could she become herself
but by stretch and pain? It was losing blood
made her skin a legendary white.

First Triptych:
Garden of Earthly Delights,
Hieronymus Bosch

These needle peaks, these green-breasted meadows
where bull and unicorn range with antelope,
contemplative elephant, exotic giraffe. Then
the astounded eye takes in the strange
monuments: in the background, a structure
recalling the delicate bones of the inner ear
pours forth blackbirds which loop
through hollow circles like belfry windows
opening nowhere, while below and nearer,
the pointed bodies of more blackbirds enter
a lopped shell, white ones flock before
the door of a smooth cave, and the stopped

mind falls farther to the bizarre
fountain in the central pool, its spire
the pistil and stamen of a stripped flower.
Bulbous-bodied creatures with long arms
climb ashore from the Waters of Bliss.
A hedge chastely separates this scene
from the meadow below, where a sallow Christ
clasps the virgin's wrist, she in the act
of falling on slender knees. He looks sideways
as if at a prurient viewer, while stupefied
Adam gapes to see the carnal sanctioned,
himself elected to this consummation.
The painter's bitter joke pierces us:
It's not sex, not desire that blights

Eden. These are barely nascent in
the hapless pair who have yet to touch. Rather, it's
the simple conviction of sin, a shrill jet
springing from the edict separating
body and soul. This Christ walls them
apart, mocks the image of the marriage priest.
They will struggle for union till they split,
wake half swallowed by demon fish,
their sexes pinned by claws. Meanwhile,
foreknowledge poses in the hieroglyphic
bodies of the animals, hooked here
biding their time in the first panel.

The Romantic Arrives Nowhere

Why don't I recognize it
for what it is? Why don't I recognize
you, its incarnation, priest of the carnal
that could suck me out of time.
Everything's religious
in its implications. Christ said
to that woman drawing water, to whom
no one else would speak: "I know you,
you're my sister. Where I know you
is home. Come home." Intimacy
is a sweet dusk you're running from,
you can't see you're falling.
At the bottom of this hill lies a meadow,
green as mother's apron, littered
with bones. We go there anyway.
The body takes us, as it should, the little death.
But afterward, we were meant to talk,
to lie folded together, two leaves
on a strong stalk that's bound to wither.
Listen to me awhile: it's not forever.
This is the communion Christ approved.
This is not romantic. To the romantic

sex is a racing engine, like the sun.
He cannot love the darkness it
dies into, a womb dark around him
even now.

Van Eyck:
The Arnolfini Wedding Portrait

Such marriages! Thank God we've outlived them:
The groom, his shaven skull like a helmet
in the great black urn of his hat, ankles in
plum-colored hose sleek as greyhounds,
holds his bride's up-turned palm like a
bleached leaf. She wears forest green
with dense smocking, her hair nunnishly hidden
under the white sails of the headdress.
In her bisque face, lashless eyes are lowered.
Four fig-sized pears cower in the gray light
of the window. The high bed looms,
red-draped and canopied, hard as a throne.

Behind them, the mirror's convex glass
repeats the scene in a cameo framed
by a black cog. The bronze chandelier
holds aloft its intricate blades. A small dog
poses at their feet, locks parted and combed,
muzzle dainty as a baby's chin,
his eyes quenched coals, even his voice
all but silenced by such careful breeding.

That Land

To be at sea and not feel the tides,
or to feel them yet hear the echo
of a surf on another shore, pounding
the memory. I think the mermaids
must have been homeless like this.
They wanted men whose bodies, whose joys
were amphibious. They wanted to walk,
to sleep in meadows bathed at dawn
only with sunlight, to touch a shoulder touched
simply by air. Everyone believed they loved
their salt heaven. The lovers who cause us to suffer
most, are filled with an infinite longing.
How can they ever swim to that land?

The Bridge

They sit in the scrubbed light
of the monastery arcade:
a man and a woman
overlooking village, black rocks, Atlantic.
A single spider weaves the sun
into maps. She looks
at her hands, shapes a few words
that hang in air like the memory
of starved children. She comes from a cold
country. Across its vast steppes
she reaches toward the man beside her
who is part of this scenery
and free. *The people*
that walked in darkness, she whispers.
Can he remember the verse?
She is like someone calling
in a dark hallway, to one who may or may not be
in the closed room at the end.
His eyes are distant
as he looks toward the sea, where the sun
turns a bridge to silk across a harbor.

Soon, she must disappear
back into the heart of cold.
But just now,

as she pulls, as from a clear dark stream,
the words like precious fish...
and in a little while, in the village
as they lie in the small bare room,
its clean flag of light at the window:
her eyes,
what her eyes say in spite of all
will be worth everything.

Daphne

I run into woods, sprouting fear
that unfurls green in my hair, shoots
from my fingers. Leaves clatter
over my branched shoulders.
Behind me, I see him, his skin
flashing gold as he runs.
He is beautiful. Feverish and vain,
he does not belong here.
Let him bask in a city of women.

Birds hammer on the dull bells of my ears.
My skin thickens in dark ribs.
Arms start their slow reach, spread out
as if to bless. It is cool here. He comes
sweating and tortured as my feet take root,
begin to grow permanently into this shade.

Crystal

It's late and I'm in bed reading.
I remember how I used to wake in the night
at sixteen, at twenty, burning
with poems, with love and nowhere
to put it. How drunk it made me, holding it,
then reaching for the pen.
Now I have to make myself get up,
go in the other room and get something
to write this down.
You're somewhere across town, I don't believe
you will ever love me. I've hurt others
like this, worse, myself. It doesn't matter.
The heart can turn to ice.

                    In every photograph
of my mother as a young woman—
the eyes, the cheekbones—there's this sense
of a fine crystal being broken down.

It Is April

And has just rained.
She sits on the back step, watches the cottonwoods
fanned on the sky, turning to etchings.
Pencil and paper in her lap,
she stares, trying to reach something
among restless brown leaves against the fence,
something with which the trees seem now about to burst,
though they do not, they come only to flower.
Something the dusk can hold for an hour one month
out of the year, before it hardens to day and night.

Soon she will rise from the drift of blank pages
and go to meet him. They will walk
and later under the weight of honesty she will say
*Wait. Listen. There was something...*and stop.
It was in another language.

In the night he will wake and watch her,
worry hollow and heavy in his eyes, watch
her neck throbbing fast like the breast of a bird.
And he will know this is not sleep.

Winter Sunlight

At times I am lifted out of myself,
sucked backward through a telescope,
the room I left
a cameo growing fainter and fainter.
In that tiny scene
I become my grandmother at seventy,
One hand searching her bodice for pins.

The first time I noticed the lacework
on the backs of my hands, the sheen
the skin takes on, losing the dull velvet,
my hand shone as from its own light.

And yesterday at the historical society tea,
the crowd, milling with hot cider and bourbon balls,
parted around a rocking chair
where an old woman sat, her bony hand
trembling to her lips, tasting the candy
carefully. The very old have their own
aura. I couldn't reach her where she sat
in the afternoon light, clear and apart
as a photograph. I knew she could disappear
and leave hardly any space, a tremor in the rocker,
a chill, like winter sunlight, on the skin.

Vigil

A spider crawls from a crack in the sill
dragging rags of web like mummy cloths,
trying each step
before the taking, careful as a pianist's
hand. Why does she come out,
looking back-from-the-dead, as winter
slams the hatches? The lower bulb of the hourglass
dwarfs the other. The eyes watch me
as she clambers over the edge, then hoists
herself back, scribbles
a glistening signature on white wood,
a few elbowed angles before she falls
to the rug, lies still,
then fingers her way out of sight
toward a litter of spider infants
that will eat her when they're big enough.

My joints ache. I want to sign a page
indelibly before winter sets its teeth
to the bone. Finches dive at the cold pane.
They must have seen that black fruit moving,
slow as Paradise, just out of reach.

Anniversary

After eighteen years she cuts iris
with the butcher knife at a single swish.
The white flowers fall in a sheaf
in the crook of her arm, fall into place
in the milk glass bowl on the dining table.
The curtains are white gauze.
Her husband in calfskin slippers
reads the paper and smokes. They do not waste words.
Outside again, she drifts
in the garden, tries to decide
if time erodes or builds up the body of things.
She studies the graying statue ringed with violets,
its lines blurred by rain, dissolving
till you cannot read the face, till the eyes
stare unfocused, the curls go lax. Their substance
feeds the earth. The iris are indestructible
after eighteen years, the garden clipped and nurtured
to perfection. The iris arrange themselves
beside the white curtains. As white, she thinks,
as salt.

The Caller

When he calls, it is late.
Stumbling through dark
you can think only *fire, war,*
so far down you've been,
asleep in the black cradle.
With a fisherman's stealth
he slides through the night,
draws you to the surface.
His voice drops its live
net across your flesh.
What he wants is as old
as icebergs, and black
at the center. This is the pull
the great ships feel, the immense
hollow. You reel as the floor

shifts. The children
are locked like clams in sleep,
the husband drifts off.
In the dark the scale sheath
glimmers. Your hair smells salt.
You tug
at the silk line of the voice.

Conundrum

Dreams must gather up everything,
black scavenger birds. The play
in which the soul is rent.
There is always someone unattainable,
someone I lost. We say
things we didn't risk that day,
wherever it was. We lie
rapt, each like a rose that has opened
to its twin in a mirror, and Cassandra

rushes in with her doomed speech:
tornadoes, murder, war. It all happens
at home, where parents and childhood
were lost. Even the dog I loved best
is there. I can't save him.
When it's over, I crawl out of the cellar,
find him in the road,
unrecognizable but for red fur.

And you, my lovers, my husband,
are fled. Who are these people
I have survived with? When I lay down
with you, I wanted to be changed,
torn apart and remade, new skin.
I wanted to do this over
and over, for practice.
Then, I thought, even dying
I will know where I am.

The Prize

When you told me of scattering
your husband's ashes
in the woods and the stream,
my tears came fast. I ran
my usual two miles, downhill
and up, and the tears flowed
like old exiles finally home.
I didn't know him, it's not her
I'm crying for. All grief
is one. You said

they were many-colored, shiny,
the way I imagine stardust,
but heavy. "They just turned over
in the water and lay down"
and I realize it's that

peace I long for, that completed love.
I run on, my breath a high whine
in the lungs. Is it the running
or the not being able to stand still?
And how long can I do it?
My bones so heavy they conduct
a terrible electricity.

Passing the women from the hospital
who walk this route leisurely at lunch,
know how to pace their lives,

I remind myself not to lose
the knack of the daily: slow down.
What's hardest is how

in this life, all moments of clarity
fade. *Like gold, LuAnn!* you said.
They shone like gold!

Upon the Waters

I.
There is a story to tell. I watch you
crossing a street in the sun
a split second before I recognize you.
Have we come so far? We sit and talk
for an hour, shaded from mid-afternoon.
Still the connection, yes, *of course*
as breath. Still the family.
I know you as well as I know myself.
But a new ease now. We may get there.
Across this rocking sea lies a meadow.

II.
We had white rooms above a back yard
full of myrtle and oak. There I made poems
many hours, made bread, letters, love.
There I could not unmake my fears.
They rose with their terrible yeast
under the carpet, under the taut cloth
of the marriage. They were not your fault.
They were ancestral and plotted
in the nerves. They meshed perfectly
with yours, which were not my fault,
which were also your birthright.

Love, the cradle is a dangerous boat.
A photo of you, born less than a month,
swaddled in a basket like Moses.
In West Texas hot as the devil's kitchen

your mother set you down on the sand.
How could you ride the surface in that light?
Your squinting face makes its own shadows.

Two years later, you sit on a couch
holding your younger brother who shrieks.
Your eyes, oh your eyes:
one larger, out-looking the other,
the infant psyche counterweighting itself
for the halving world.

Meanwhile I flourished among irises,
cushioned by my grandmother, a deep grief
that never told itself in tale or anger.
Only later, in senility,
did her black fears birth themselves
like old stone gods: unwedded pregnancy,
throngs of strangers reaching their hands.
I was twelve when the light on the fields
went vacant.

Then adolescence. The storm of sex
racking the blood, the air too thick to breathe
and no one, Father, Mother, no one
on the horizon, Mother, Father, the perilous straits,
the desert mirages that overcome.
We were twinned in our desires early on.

So I took your hand. We went
to a ballet, we watched
a dance of impossible grace and balance.

The stage shimmered like water. And we kept
following, even into marriage,
its easy smiles and silk roses.
We battened down our fears, we set sail.
There was work to do, a whole world
to chart.

        But the horizon
would not change, the weather was fixed
as a ship in a bottle. Where were the islands
of fluting birds, the miraculous changes?
Was there not enough water, did I not know
how to drink, how to cup my hands
and take salt? Sometimes it seemed
we were adrift on a mirror, so much light
I couldn't see. My eyes craved darkness,
my body longed
to plunge in an element I couldn't find.

One day I let down a small raft,
left you to steer alone. There were no stars
we could map. An endless rain
roughened the sea like wool. Each of us
became smaller then, diminishing points
on the two sides of a slowly widening angle.

We are almost past the time of that journey,
know each other now as one might know
a friend come back from death. Haven't we
come back, don't we believe

that selves which die feed those which
survive? Aren't we learning how to row?

III.
In Raphael's *Miraculous Draught of the Fishes*
the balance overwhelms. The tiny boats
are already dangerously laden with fish,
yet James and John bend over, rounded muscles
straining at the nets, while Simon Peter
kneels with folded hands to the seated Christ—
He could put out his arm and touch the shore.
How those anxious figures lean and strain
toward him, yet do not think of falling!
Nor does the eye fall, bathed in the light
of muted reds, blues, and gold. The sea's color
flows into the sky's. On the opposite bank
a small crowd has gathered from the blue-domed town:
mothers with infants, workmen throwing off robes.
It is a holiday because of the harvest.
They gaze excitedly at the thrashing surface,
though not at the awe-struck fishermen.
A few appear to be watching four swans
that preen and bathe in the midground.
The sea stains their plumage pale blue.
In buoyant grace they ride apart
from miracle, abundance, and doubt,
from the desires of those who go upon the waters.

Icarus Swims

for B.

Think of it, love, what if the tales, the price-
less paintings, all were wrong. What if they lied
because the old cults thrived on sacrifice
and tragedy, and had to say he died.

What if the sun was midwife at a birth,
melting the wax, letting him plunge naked
to the christening sea, with infant mirth,
with joy amphibious. So much is staked

on our courage to recast the myths.
I love you, sear you, cut you loose to fall
worse than Adam, guiltless. I do this
for selfish life, for passion's fundamental

mystery: We must save ourselves, and him.
Imagine it. *Imagine it,* and *swim.*

IV

DAYBREAK

The Old Reapers

I would like to gather my powers
as the old reapers stooped to gather wheat
by the armful. Draw up a stiff gold sheaf
in the brittle sun. Bind it tight.
Stand back, washed in sweat, hands
stiff with the leather of labor.

The pain in the hands drops deeper
like small ships drifting down
unwinding the long echo of their groans.
The hands lift the sheaves, lean them carefully
in shocks. At dusk
the field is a poem of primitive huts.

Sonogram

I slide off my panelled jeans,
tie the hospital gown behind my neck.
Its soft faded print reminds me
of feed-sack aprons my grandmother made:
something familiar in this sterile room
where, seeing your face, I will be born
all over.

        I've carried you four months
in the world where things happen to us.
While you're flutter-kicking in suspension,
I'm swimming in the past: her aprons
that cradled eggs, my mother who writes
"Remember the fat lady at the fair
when you said—not knowing she could hear—
It's just her dress, she's not that fat.
Remember?" She's not sure what to say
about you yet. She's not quite ready.
Was she ready for me? Was I ready
that first day in our new house, the two of us
trembling in dust, in the sun's arms?
Its June face flooded the window,
a yellow apple we'd bitten. In a few hours,
the time it takes a sperm to swim six inches,
you were done, begun, new link
in the old chain.

The technician, refusing to talk, works
nearly an hour gliding the blunt sensor
over the blown skin of my belly.

I search the screen till my eyes wear out
and I imagine a face, a smile
in the gray nether place of dough kneaded
and kneaded in the palm of sound.
Methodically she types: *head, heart, hand*
and finally points. A tiny ghost face surfaces,
a thin arm and fist. *Boy,* she thinks,
but suddenly you turn on your stomach,
curl like a snail from the squalls of sound.
She flips the switch. You can keep on
dream-sleeping another five months
till you drop into a stranger element, begin
to understand the linkages, the gaps,
the heart's bobbles as it sinks and rises
sounding after sounding. Here are some
truths for the waking dream you'll burst into:

I am your mother, this is your father.
We both have mothers and fathers. And the sun—
old heart-throb—flames as it sinks,
blazes rising. Goes dead white at noon
and keeps on.

Echolalia

for Luke

Your first birthday. I'm up early
steeping tea, saving a quiet hour
before you begin your funny answer
to the rooster, the hungry lambs, the cranky geese
who yammer through the fog outside your window.
I'll hear your soft hoots and crows,
my mother-brain suspended, listening
as you sing yourself awake a good half-hour
while the rest of me gets on with words.
Language is my edge on entropy—
my last hope, I used to think.
Now there's *your* language, truer than any
you'll ever speak: It translates nothing,
is the pure voice of the nascent soul,
your mind's *croissance*, your natural joy
tongued forth moment by moment like new
leaves. *Knowing* this
comes later, when tongue and brain
have learned to struggle with what they mean.
Now, you fit the world perfectly, no space
between you and its laughter. Blessed state,

the primal wit remembering before the Word
what the poet labors to bring forth:
harmony incarnate, the first Yes.

Trust

for M.

...a single shawl
Wrapped tightly round us...
A light, a power, the miraculous influence
—Wallace Stevens

And sometimes, after the "intensest rendezvous,"
your arms may find they encircle air,
or, if I am there, may find (your arms
will know) my soul is not, has gone somewhere

secret, or maybe just apart. One wren
of a pair will occasionally glide to a separate
branch. Who understands this
but God, who gave things their discreteness.

Never mind. Trust
the miraculous influence: Was it not
a universe? And has its sphere
more of the finite than the infinite? Trust

what we are given: these vast bright waters'
buoyancy, this single-shawled starship's thrust.

Here Face Down

And here face down beneath the sun
And here upon earth's noonward height
To feel the always coming on
The always rising of the night...
                    —Archibald MacLeish

It's early morning. I'm reading *Walden*,
"Winter Animals," while my husband sleeps
and our son wakes slowly to greet
the sun on the sheep farm through his windows.
He likes the arpeggios it plays
through naked *ailanthus*, "trees of heaven," on his walls
lined with color wildlife photographs.
Outside, the trees speak in tongues.
This is their glory week. Thoreau hears
"the cracking of the ground by the frost,
as if some one had driven a team against
my door, and in the morning would find
a crack in the earth a quarter of a mile long..."
Yet winter is not nearly so deep at Walden
as here, Virginia, 1988.
We're warm as mice in a nest, and overhead
the delicate placenta of the ozone
thins out like blown glass before the sun.
In Antarctica, the penguin nations
may find their tailored coats too warm,
great whales freeze in waters blown
empty of krill by ultra-violence—
before the baby reaches twenty-one.

What coat will protect him from that summer—
green shoot love fired into the future.
Here sits his mother, coaxing her poem
like a weak candle, though it's late
for songs, even lamentations.

Henry David, when will the Visitor come?
Does the "old settler and original proprietor"
still reside in this desperate wood
that grows the wilder as it is cut down?
Or have we routed him, is there no one
but ourselves, this inarticulate season?

I let words rest, pick up the camera,
step out in crackling frost to catch the leaves
repeating the sun in brilliant dialects.
May they teach us how to speak and dress
in ruined Eden, before our nakedness.

The Hart

At times, as if for no reason, a hart
springs into the landscape. The sky is
flint-gray and packed down like that excelsior
made of undyed lint. And through your window
over the edge of a slope strewn with leaves,
the hart appears. However you name him,
however quaint and disused the name,
he is yours. Not his whom you loved
too much, poured yourself out on as upon sand.
Nor the ghost's you have danced with for years
to the frayed end of strength. Having survived
these, and in spite of winter coming,
he is yours as surely as the future.
He stands there, hide the color of tough oak leaves,
having gone for days without food. You know now
you will never let him go entirely from the eye's
tether. Already the sun,
a live coal just visible in the ashen sky,
ignites his flank, a ripple of warmth
blesses him.

River Dolphins:
Ganges, Indus, Amazon, La Plata, Yangtze

Smaller in body and brain
than their flashy prodigious cousins,
and ghost-colored: pink, ecru, silver, pewter—
though colors do not exist for them
who have almost outgrown the need for light,
in turbid waters the bright coin of the lens
all but disappearing. Left here
when the strange-shaped seas departed,
what compass, what obscure throb of the landscape
said *home,* so that hearing shaped itself
to river bottoms, the child-sized body to swim
on its side, finger-scalloped flipper grazing mud

while the world changed, vast chunks drifting
across time.

In flood season, some of them swim among trees
in the Chinese forests, the branches overhead
alive with the yammer of birds and monkeys.
How many creatures, how many man-tribes
have come and gone in dolphin time?
What do they know, these elder children,
what blood wisdom inscribed in fiber and
cell-cloister, secrets of the art
of staying on.

On the Lower Surface

Watching rare spotted dolphins
roll and whirl above him, a diver
lies with his camera
flat on the sandy bottom. One
with ragged dorsal and enigmatic smile
settles slowly downward near the man
till he rests belly-flat on the sand.
Intrigued, the man stands

                    and the dolphin
with great effort, as if he believes
this experiment worthwhile, and
slowly—now he is not playing
or this play is of a higher order—
the dolphin stands,
his blade tail nudging the sand
like a fine-honed foot. He faces the man.
Think of his brain at full bloom
before we began to remember, of what the two brains
have flowered toward: This

is a conversation. The man
shifts his camera, stuttering.
His body lightens, the awkward limbs
graceful in this element.
Inside the mask, he sheds
tears of laughter for the swaying
dolphin, untranslatable hope,
sea water the mother of blood.

Sumeria

They gave us the words for *abyss*
and *Eden,* flung out like winged seeds
from that first culture. Set lapis
in bronze they invented, for beads,
toilet boxes, palace walls. Gave us
wheeled chariots, commerce, the ziggurat,
the first known empire, the myth
of the Flood, the irrigation ditch
embroidering barley fields and groves of date palms.
Even their government was noble, early on:
councils of elders choosing one temporary
ruler after another, punishments mild,
mostly fines; monogamy; male *and* female
scribes. Above all else, the earliest

writing, a phonetic alphabet. After millennia,
the brain able to dissect language to its
atomic parts, the table of elements
from which civilization bursts.
Christians wrongly have it they were
confounded at the Tower of Babel,
their stolen fire squelched by a jealous God
who well might fear this seed, this *ergal.*
Picture the scribes, pregnant in long robes,
the fluent reed imprinting the brain's schema
on doughy cakes of clay: the word
made flesh. So that despite time's maw,
memory would not disappear. Idea
taking root, the Eden of possibility
burgeoning on the edge of abyss.
Summative, consummate. All this.

Leonardo: *The Adoration*

> ...the world...streaming
> In the electrolysis of love.
> —Kenneth Rexroth

What has held me so long
before this painting? The awe-stricken crowd
cascade like swept leaves at her feet,
a few small angels among them blossoming
light. And the wild heads of the horses,
their eyes whorled with fear, rise
like the spume of a beaten sea. War
and strife cloud the distance,
held off from this center as if by
centrifugal force. At the still eye,
mother and child, their bodies brushed
with light. The tree lifts above them
its dense speech.

Unfinished? or perhaps
the way to tell a story more than the sum
of men and events. As if it were not
the clustered, turbulent figures
he wanted to show, not these at all,
but the molecular dance, the invisible
stream that pulses in this scene,
the godstuff itself. To see—not through
but *into*—every filled thing, even
the paint and the tense bristles

remembering their roots in skin
as they wash over all a gold light.
So that, in this dusky, troubled pond,
great doors swing wide:

There is the tree
drinking and speaking the pure *I am,*
milk that feeds all hungers
rising through pores of ancient canvas
in a thousand springs.

Materia Maternae

The sun has passed the horizon, climbed behind
clouds banked smooth as a blue-gray bowl.
Just under its rim, a streak of coral.
My mother had a bowl like this
she used to mix chocolate cake in.
The blue paint was wearing from the milky glass.
Looking through from inside out,
it was just this color,
a quiet, closed sky transmitting light,
the rim a faded orange. I used to believe
I could walk from our back porch
and touch the wall of the sky, put my palm
on that sheer curve upward to the blue vault.
If I just walked far enough.
That we lived in an inverted dome,
sound as a fish bowl, didn't bother me then.

When did it happen? The walls were blown away.
My heart has a cleft every lover widens.
I see right through the sky now,
even in daytime:
the black stuff shot with sunlight,
the burst, impassioned stars.

Vessel

for D.

Maybe it's almost finished, saying "I."
A wall of light, a stoppedness
every hour of the self, like the blinding radiance
of an open door.

              And we, miles apart,
are losing even the need for words.
I felt you here last night when the trees
gathered in their dark nets the sky's
purple trout. How we long to be
drawn up—but not

yet. At last we are learning
to hold. I think I could become a tree
whose leaves are both its body
and its poems. All day the sun's voice
pours into the translucent vessel.

The Man Beneath the Tundra

for Luke

He lies in a cradle of ice
in the Arctic earth,
sailor from an expedition lost
more than a century ago. The researchers
pour water over the block that fills
his coffin. Slowly, slowly, the face
surfaces: eyes open, mouth pulled
into a grin by starvation,
the skin leather-brown. Yet
he is not frightening, looks almost
friendly, as though he doesn't mind,
even welcomes this intrusion.
They lift the loosening arms, examine
his quaint clothing. I peer at the underside

of my fascination: Don't we all
want to surface through the ice
of our cautiousness, to be lifted
by gentle, knowledgeable men and women
who say *of course, this was the problem,
here is the explanation.*

Don't we want to see ourselves
delivered from the glacier of grief
that swept us under, whose dimensions,
direction, and origin we could never
fathom? Thawed, freed, and smiling
hello, hello to the kind doctors
or angels or better yet, our tomorrow's
selves, those hard-borne children,
faces stamped with our clear, untroubled
features. *Yes, you did,* they say,
in spite of the climate. Yes, we can.

About the Author

LUANN KEENER has a Master of Fine Arts in creative writing from the University of Arkansas and teaches at Virginia Polytechnic Institute and State University. Her work has been widely published in literary journals, including *The Greensboro Review, Northwest Review, Southern Poetry Review, Chelsea,* and *Quarterly West.* She is the recipient of numerous awards, most recently the Irene Leach Poetry Prize, the Hackney Poetry Award, the Chelsea Prize for Poetry, a MacDowell Colony Creative Writing Residency, and a Writers at Work Award in Poetry. She lives in Salem, Virginia, with her son.

Selected Titles from Award-Winning CALYX Books

Natalie on the Street by Ann Nietzke. A day-by-day account of the author's relationship with an elderly homeless woman who lived on the streets of Nietzke's central Los Angeles neighborhood.
ISBN 0-934971-41-2, $14.95, paper; ISBN 0-934971-42-0, $24.95, cloth.

Light in the Crevice Never Seen by Haunani-Kay Trask. The first book of poetry by an indigenous Hawaiian to be published in North America. It is a revelation about a Native woman's love for her land, and the inconsolable grief and rage that come from its destruction.
ISBN 0-934971-37-4, $11.95, paper; ISBN 0-934971-38-2, $21.95, cloth.

The Violet Shyness of Their Eyes: Notes from Nepal by Barbara J. Scot. A moving account of a western woman's transformative sojourn in Nepal as she reaches mid-life. PNBA Book Award.
ISBN 0-934971-35-8, $14.95, paper; ISBN 0-934971-36-6, $24.95, cloth.

Open Heart by Judith Mickel Sornberger. An elegant collection of poetry rooted in a woman's relationships with family, ancestors, and the world.
ISBN 0-934971-31-5, $9.95, paper; ISBN 0-934971-32-3, $19.95, cloth.

Raising the Tents by Frances Payne Adler. A personal and political volume of poetry, documenting a woman's discovery of her voice. Finalist, WESTAF Book Awards.
ISBN 0-934971-33-1, $9.95, paper; ISBN 0-934971-34-x, $19.95, cloth.

Killing Color by Charlotte Watson Sherman. These compelling, mythical short stories by a gifted storyteller delicately explore the African-American experience. Washington Governor's Award.
ISBN 0-934971-17-X, $9.95, paper; ISBN 0-934971-18-8, $19.95, cloth.

Mrs. Vargas and the Dead Naturalist by Kathleen Alcalá. Fourteen stories set in Mexico and the Southwestern U.S., written in the tradition of magical realism.
ISBN 0-934971-25-0, $9.95, paper; ISBN 0-934971-26-9, $19.95, cloth.

Black Candle: Poems about Women from India, Pakistan, and Bangladesh by Chitra Divakaruni. Lyrical and honest poems that chronicle significant moments in the lives of South Asian women. Gerbode Award.
ISBN 0-934971-23-4, $9.95, paper; ISBN 0-934971-24-2, $19.95 cloth.

Ginseng and Other Tales from Manila by Marianne Villanueva. Poignant short stories set in the Philippines. Manila Critic's Circle National Literary Award Nominee.
ISBN 0-934971-19-6, $9.95, paper; ISBN 0-934971-20-X, $19.95, cloth.

Colophon

The type for *Color Documentary* was set in Optima.

Design and typeset by ImPrint Services, Corvallis, Oregon.